101 Facts About Our World

101 FACTS ABOUT

TROPICAL RAIN FORESTS

Julia Barnes

Gareth Stevens Publishing
A WORLD ALMANAC EDUCATION GROUP COMPANY

Please visit our web site at: www.garethstevens.com
For a free color catalog describing Gareth Stevens Publishing's
list of high-quality books and multimedia programs,
call 1-800-542-2595 (USA) or 1-800-387-3178 (Canada).
Gareth Stevens Publishing's fax: (414) 332-3567.

Library of Congress Cataloging-in-Publication Data available upon request
from publisher. Fax (414) 336-0157 for the attention of the Publishing
Records Department.

ISBN 0-8368-3710-X

This North American edition first published in 2004 by
Gareth Stevens Publishing
A World Almanac Education Group Company
330 West Olive Street, Suite 100
Milwaukee, WI 53212 USA

This U.S. edition copyright © 2004 by Gareth Stevens, Inc. Original edition © 2003 by First
Stone Publishing. First published by First Stone Publishing, 4/5 The Marina, Harbour
Road, Lydney, Gloucestershire, GL15 5ET, United Kingdom. Additional end matter © 2004
by Gareth Stevens, Inc.

First Stone Series Editor: Claire Horton-Bussey
First Stone Designer: Rob Benson
Geographical consultant: Miles Ellison
Gareth Stevens Editors: Catherine Gardner and JoAnn Early Macken

Photographs © Oxford Scientific Films Ltd

Printed in Hong Kong through Printworks Int. Ltd

1 2 3 4 5 6 7 8 9 07 06 05 04 03

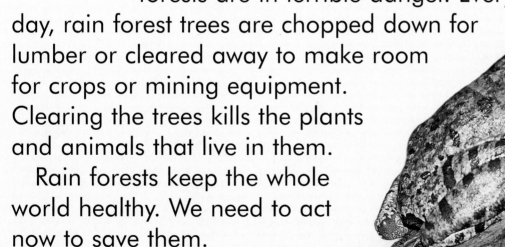

Tropical rain forests are among the most precious natural treasures on Earth. So many different kinds of plants and trees grow in warm, wet rain forests that it is impossible to count them all. Amazing animals live at every level and make use of every part of the rain forest, from the long branches and leaves stretching toward the sun to the dark, damp ground below.

No other places on Earth have a richer variety of wildlife and plants – yet rain forests are in terrible danger. Every day, rain forest trees are chopped down for lumber or cleared away to make room for crops or mining equipment. Clearing the trees kills the plants and animals that live in them.

Rain forests keep the whole world healthy. We need to act now to save them.

MAJOR TROPICAL RAIN FORESTS

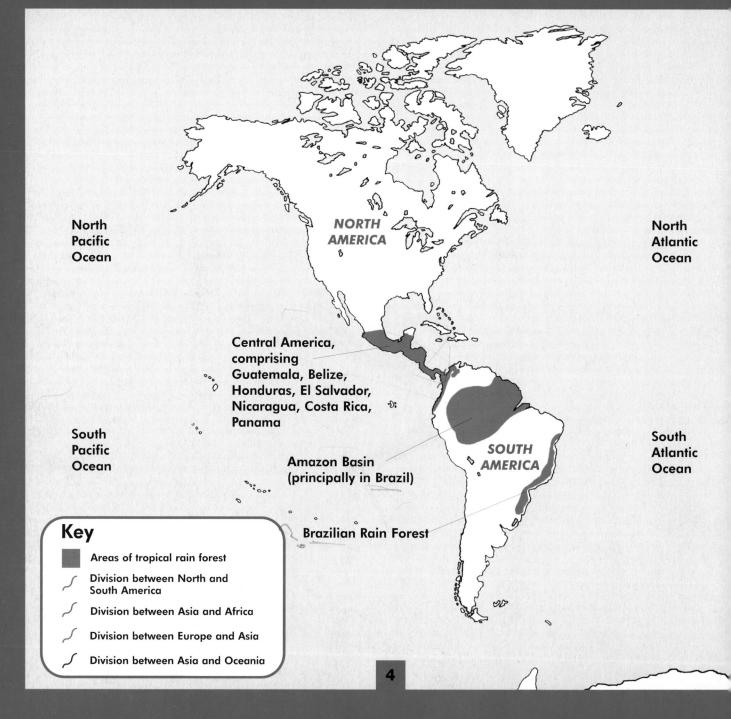

North Pacific Ocean

NORTH AMERICA

North Atlantic Ocean

Central America, comprising Guatemala, Belize, Honduras, El Salvador, Nicaragua, Costa Rica, Panama

South Pacific Ocean

Amazon Basin (principally in Brazil)

SOUTH AMERICA

South Atlantic Ocean

Brazilian Rain Forest

Key

Areas of tropical rain forest

Division between North and South America

Division between Asia and Africa

Division between Europe and Asia

Division between Asia and Oceania

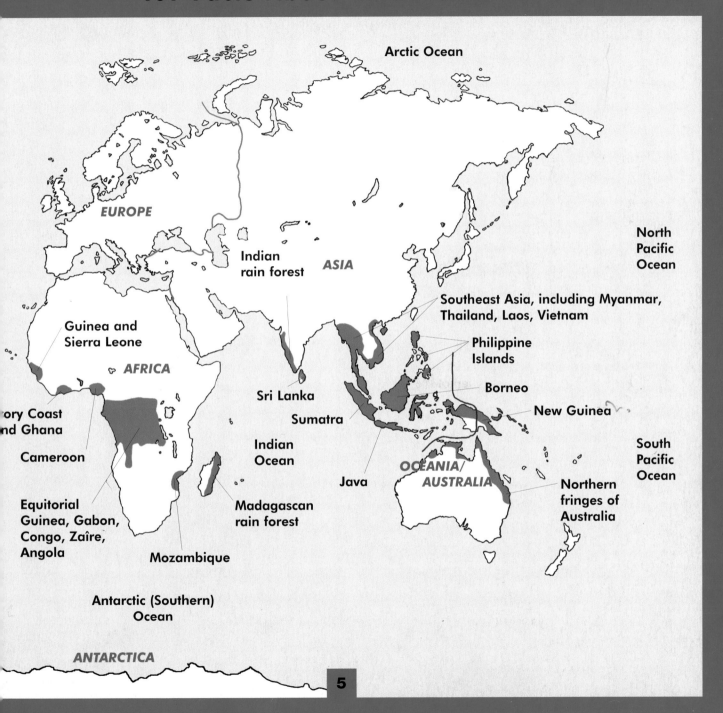

Arctic Ocean

EUROPE

Indian
rain forest

ASIA

North
Pacific
Ocean

Southeast Asia, including Myanmar,
Thailand, Laos, Vietnam

Guinea and
Sierra Leone

AFRICA

Philippine
Islands

Sri Lanka

Borneo

ory Coast
nd Ghana

Sumatra

New Guinea

Cameroon

Indian
Ocean

South
Pacific
Ocean

OCEANIA/
AUSTRALIA

Java

Equitorial
Guinea, Gabon,
Congo, Zaîre,
Angola

Madagascan
rain forest

Northern
fringes of
Australia

Mozambique

Antarctic (Southern)
Ocean

ANTARCTICA

1 Tropical rain forests have given us many of the medicines we need and the foods we eat, but we still have much to learn about these amazing places.

2 Steamy rain forests of dense trees and wildlife (right) covered much of our planet tens of millions of years ago, forming one of Earth's oldest **biomes**.

3 Today, these forests remain mostly around the middle of the globe in parts of the world that have a **tropical climate**, including West Africa, southeast Asia, the Pacific islands, northern and eastern South America, and Central America.

4 The Amazon Basin in South America is the world's largest rain forest at 2.7 million square miles (7 million square kilometers).

5 In a tropical rain forest, the **temperature** and hours of daylight do not change with the seasons. It stays about 80° Fahrenheit (27° Celsius) every day.

6 At least 80 inches (200 centimeters) of rain fall in a tropical rain forest each year.

7 The warm, wet weather creates ideal living conditions for plants and animals. More than half of the **species** in the world make their homes in tropical rain forests.

8 Over one hundred different species of trees might grow in 2.5 acres (1 hectare) of tropical rain forest.

9 Each 2.5 acres (1 ha) of the rain forest may contain only one or two trees of each species.

10 In rain forests, ants, butterflies, beetles, and other insects outnumber other species.

11 Tropical rain forests have a wide variety of mammals. Some of them, such as bats, monkeys, and sloths, live high in the trees. Others, such as tapirs and jaguars, stay closer to the ground.

12 Brightly-colored frogs (left), toads, lizards, snakes, and other reptiles and amphibians hide in the tree branches of a rain forest.

13 The crowned pigeon (above right) lives in New Guinea. Unusual birds as tiny as **nectar**-sipping hummingbirds and as large as monkey-eating eagles are among the many birds that nest in tropical rain forests.

14 It is difficult to see through the tangle of tree branches and plants.

Animals must call out to find friends and scare enemies.

17 Every morning and evening, troops of howler monkeys begin their strange wails. Their calls may warn one troop to stay out of another troop's area.

15 Tropical rain forests are filled with the sounds of croaking frogs, chirping insects, chattering monkeys, and singing birds.

16 The howler monkey from South America (right) may be the noisiest of all the rain forest animals. Its call travels for miles (km).

20 Just below the overstory is the **canopy** layer, where most of the tall, straight trees branch out (left).

21 The canopy is a continuous layer of branches and green leaves that stretch out to reach the bright sun.

18 A tropical rain forest can be divided into four different layers.

19 At the very top is the overstory, where the **emergent trees** grow above the others. This layer is windy and dry compared to lower layers of the rain forest.

22 Each leaf in the canopy is angled so that it receives as much sunlight as possible.

23 Some leaves have a special joint at the base of the stalk so they can twist and follow the sun as it moves from east to west.

24 The leaves may have waxy coatings or special shapes to let rain drip off them quickly.

25 Most of the animals that live in the rain forest make their homes in the canopy.

26 The parrot family has at least 300 different species. Many of these species, such as the black-headed caique (below left), live in the rain forest canopy, where they feed on fruit, seeds, and nuts.

27 The most brilliant of the rain forest parrots are the macaws (right). These birds have bright colors, long tail feathers, and sharp, curved beaks.

28 The most ferocious bird in the rain forest is the giant eagle.

29 Each tropical rain forest has its own species of giant eagle: the monkey-eating eagle in southeast Asia, the harpy eagle in South America (below), and the crowned eagle in Africa.

30 Flying above the canopy, giant eagles spot smaller birds or mammals and then dive into the branches to attack.

31 Rain forest eagles have sharp, strong **talons** to carry their **prey** back to their nests. They nest on big platforms of twigs in the tallest trees.

32 The toucan (above) from the Amazon rain forest is known for its giant beak. The toucan's beak is about one-third as long as its body, but it is surprisingly lightweight.

33 Toucans cannot fly as far as most rain forest birds can. They hop from branch to branch.

34 Flying is a good way to travel in a tropical rain forest. Most birds and bats easily swoop through the thick canopy.

35 Not all animals can fly, but they still try. They have **adaptations** that let them glide from tree to tree.

36 The flying lemur, or colugo, is at home in trees in Malaysia (below). It may look as if it flies, but this mammal really glides.

39 Flying tree frogs (left) of the rain forests in Costa Rica are also adapted to life in the trees. They have webbing around their hands and feet that acts like a parachute when the frogs jump.

37 The flying lemur has skin that stretches from its neck to its front feet and from its front feet to its back feet. This skin catches the breeze like a sail.

40 Flying tree frogs take long leaps from tall trees and then glide to safe landing places.

38 With its arms and legs outstretched, the flying lemur can glide about 230 feet (70 meters) before it lands on another tree branch.

41 Some tropical rain forest animals that cannot fly or glide are able to move through the canopy by climbing and leaping.

43 Like people, monkeys have hands with fingers, but they also use their feet and toes to grip and hold things.

44 Most monkeys also have a tail (below), which they can use like an extra hand as they swing from branch to branch.

42 Monkeys are some of the world's best climbers, and many different species make their homes in tropical rain forests. The white-faced saki (above) is a South American monkey. It lives in trees and eats fruits and leaves.

45 Orangutans (left), members of the ape family, live in rain forests in Borneo and Sumatra.

46 Most monkeys and apes live in groups, but orangutans live alone among the trees. Grown males stay away from others, and females care for the young.

47 Today, few orangutans are left in the wild. Humans have hunted many and taken over their forests.

48 Gorillas roam the African rain forests. These powerful animals are the biggest apes (below).

49 Gorillas are gentle creatures that eat plants and fruit. They do not often need to use their awesome strength.

50 Monkeys that live in the canopy are safe from most of the rain forest's hunters, but not all of them.

51 The tree-dwelling cats – margays (above) from South America and clouded leopards from Asia – hunt birds, squirrels, and monkeys.

53 Sloths, which eat leaves, spend most of their time hanging upside down in tree branches.

54 To hang on, sloths have claws like hooks and legs and arms like bony hangers.

55 Sloths' hair grows in the opposite direction of most animals so that rain runs off their bodies as they hang upside down.

52 Sloths (above) of South America are neither quick nor **agile**, but these mammals are perfectly adapted for the conditions of tropical rain forests.

56 At night, the fruit bats, such as the flying fox from Australia, (left) come out to eat. They hang upside down from branches, eating fruit and dropping seeds to the ground.

57 The dropped seeds begin new plant life on the forest floor.

58 Above the ground and underneath the canopy in a tropical rain forest is a layer called the understory (right).

59 The canopy blocks most light, making the understory dim. Palms and tree ferns survive in these gloomy conditions.

60 Some plants in the understory have found ways to survive by growing on trees.

61 Climbing plants called lianas grow up from the ground to reach the canopy.

62 The long, tough stems of lianas are like ropes. Animals use them to climb up and down the trees.

63 Orchids (right) and bromeliad plants (below left) anchor themselves to the tree branches in the understory. Their roots dangle in the air to take in moisture.

64 In the leaves of bromeliad plants, water forms pools, which are used by poison arrow frogs (above right) from South America. These frogs live on the lowest layer of the rain forest, called the forest floor.

65 Poison arrow frogs climb off the floor to the pools in plant leaves when their young hatch from eggs into tadpoles.

66 Female frogs carry the tadpoles up the trunks of trees until they find leaves that are full of water.

67 The tiny poison arrow tadpoles are lowered into the pools and left there to feed on insect eggs and develop.

68 Some plants, such as Venus flytraps, eat insects. Their sticky leaves wrap around any insects that land on them.

69 Pitcher plants have another way to trap insects. Their jug-shaped leaves (right) can collect water. Insects that fall into the leaves drown and are broken down to make food for the plant.

70 The top layer of a rain forest is windy. In the lower layers, the wind is blocked. It cannot help spread pollen, the powdery grains needed to produce new plants.

71 Plants and trees in a tropical rain forest need animals to carry and spread pollen for them.

72 Birds, bats, and insects, including butterflies (left), help spread pollen. They visit flowers to drink the sugary nectar and get covered in the tiny grains of pollen.

73 As the animals move from flower to flower, the pollen rubs off. When a flower has been **pollinated** in this way, it can produce seeds or fruit for new growth.

74 Many of the plants in the rain forest can help people as well as

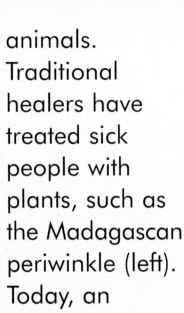

animals. Traditional healers have treated sick people with plants, such as the Madagascan periwinkle (left). Today, an increasing number of rain forest plants are being used in modern medicines.

75 The forest floor (right) is a damp and dark place. Very little of the light that falls on the canopy makes it through the leaves to the forest floor.

76 Mosses and ferns are among the few plants that can survive the wet and dark conditions.

77 The forest floor is covered with leaves and fruits that have fallen from the trees. At this level of the tropical rain forest, plant material begins to decay, or break down, immediately.

78 A pine tree needle takes years to decay in a cold forest. An oak leaf in a warmer forest decays in about one year. In a tropical rain forest, the process is faster.

79 A leaf in a tropical rain forest decays totally within just six weeks of landing on the ground.

80 The **leaf litter** on the rain forest floor is rich in nutrients, but just below the surface, the soil is poor in quality.

81 If a rain forest is cleared of trees and used for crops, nutrients in the soil are used quickly, and the land becomes useless.

82 Few large animals live on the floor of a tropical rain forest. They have a difficult time finding enough food there.

83 Deer, wild pigs called peccaries, and tapirs (left) **forage** on the forest floor. They eat roots and any small plants they can find.

84 In Africa, wild hogs (right) often run on the ground behind gibbons that swing in the branches of the canopy. The hogs eat the fruit that these small apes drop along the way.

85 Bongos (left), which live in Africa, get the minerals they need by eating pieces of trees that were struck by lightning.

86 Tropical rain forest animals must be on the lookout for jaguars that silently hunt for prey among the trees.

animals and other insects. Termites and ants march in long columns, looking for food and building material for their huge nests.

89 Rain forests are still home to traditional groups of people who make a living by hunting animals and growing crops.

87 The rain forest floor may not have many big animals, but it has plenty of insects. Among the many different insects are South American grasshoppers (above) and giant Brazilian cockroaches (below right).

90 Traditional people of the rain forest include the Veddah (above

88 Beetles feed on the bodies of dead

right), who live in Sri Lanka, and the Yanomami, who live in South America and were found by the outside world only fifty years ago.

91 Some groups of people have lived undisturbed in rain forests for hundreds of years.

92 In the last hundred years, about ninety traditional groups of people have lost their homes in the Amazon rain forest.

93 Modern people cut down many trees to make furniture and build homes. They also clear huge areas of land so they can use it for growing crops or for grazing their cattle and other livestock.

destruction continues, it will be a disaster for life all over our planet.

96 Tropical rain forests are unique places. If people destroy them, some species lose the only homes they have.

94 Drilling for oil and mining for iron ore, gold, and other minerals have destroyed even more parts of the rain forests.

97 Deforestation has destroyed some rain forest species and threatens the survival of others.

95 The destruction of rain forests is called deforestation (above). If this

98 Plants that could help make new medicines are dying before scientists can study them.

99 Most important, rain forests act like lungs for the planet. Rain forest plants take in and store **carbon dioxide**. They let out clean, pure **oxygen**, which animals need to breathe.

100 By exchanging carbon dioxide and oxygen, rain forests help counteract the **greenhouse effect**, which could harm the whole planet.

101 Rain forests are a major **resource** for all of us. We must save them before it is too late.

🍃 Glossary

adaptations: features that make survival easier in a certain place.

agile: able to move easily.

biomes: types of communities in nature with conditions that support certain kinds of plant and animal life.

canopy: the second layer from the top of a rain forest.

carbon dioxide: a gas in the air that is used by plants to produce oxygen, which we breathe.

emergent trees: the tallest rain forest trees that grow higher than the canopy layer.

forage: to search for.

greenhouse effect: a process in which gases in the atmosphere absorb infrared rays from Earth and maintain or raise temperature.

leaf litter: rotting leaves that are found on the forest floor.

nectar: a sweet, sugary substance produced by flowers.

oxygen: a gas in the air that we need to breathe.

pollinated: fertilized by pollen so a new plant can grow.

prey: animals that are hunted by others for food.

resource: a thing that has value.

species: types of plants or animals that are alike in many ways.

talons: a hunting bird's claws.

temperature: a measurement of heat or cold.

tropical climate: warm weather and heavy rainfall, mainly found in areas located around the middle of the world.

More Books to Read

***Crafts for Kids Who Are
Wild About Rainforests***
Kathy Ross
(Millbrook Press)

***Rain Forest Worlds
(Discovery Guides* series)**
Rosie McCormick
(Two-Can Publishing)

***Rain Forest (Look Closer* series)**
Barbara Taylor
(DK Publishing)

***Rainforests (Learn About* series)**
Jen Green
(Lorenz Books)

Web Sites

The Amazing Rain Forest
www.arborday.org/programs/
RainForestRescue.html

Rain Forest Report Card
www.bsrsi.msu.edu/rfrc/
home.html

Enchanting Rainforests
www.enchantedlearning.com/
subjects/rainforest/

Rainforest Action Network
www.ran.org/kids_action/

To find additional web sites, use a reliable search engine to find one or more of the following keywords: **Amazon, rain forest, tropical forest.**

 # Index

apes 16, 17, 25

bats 8, 13, 18, 22
birds 8, 9, 11, 12, 13, 22

canopy 10, 11, 14, 17, 19,
  20, 23, 25
clouded leopards 17

deforestation 28, 29

emergent trees 10

flying lemur 13, 14
forest floor 20, 23, 24, 25, 26
frogs 8, 9, 14, 20, 21

gorillas 17

insects 8, 9, 10, 21, 22, 26

jaguars 8, 25

lianas 20

margays 17
medicines 6, 23, 28
monkeys 9, 15, 16, 17

orangutans 16

plants 3, 7, 8, 19, 20, 21,
  22, 23, 25, 29

rainfall 7
reptiles 8

sloths 8, 18

tapirs 8, 25
traditional people 26, 27

understory 19, 20

wild hogs 25